EVERYTHING IS SUPER GREAT

by **Stephen Brown**

STEELE SPRING
STAGE RIGHTS
www.stagerights.com

EVERYTHING IS SUPER GREAT

For all stage performance inquiries, please contact:

Steele Spring Stage Rights
3845 Cazador Street
Los Angeles, CA 90065
(323) 739-0413
www.stagerights.com

Artwork by: Muse Graphic Design

EVERYTHING IS SUPER GREAT

ORIGINAL PRODUCTION BILLINGS

Everything is Super Great had a co-world premiere in New York and Florida.

DEVELOPMENT

Everything is Super Great was originally written in Primary Stages ESPA School and was developed under the dramaturg Tessa LaNeve in their ESPA Drills program.

Everything is Super Great was developed as part of MCC's PlayLabs, New York City, NY.

Everything is Super Great was a 2014 Winner of the GAP Prize and developed at Aurora Theatre Company, Berkeley, CA.

NEW YORK PRODUCTION

Everything Is Super Great (a comedy about what's missing) opened on November 22, 2019 at 59E59 Theaters and was produced by New Light Theatre Project (Sarah Norris, Artistic Director; Michael Aguirre, Producing Director) in association with Stable Cable Lab Co. (Lisa Jill Anderson, Artistic Director).

Creative & Production Team:
Written by Stephen Brown
Directed by Sarah Norris
Casting by Gama Valle
Scenic Design by Brian Dudkiewicz
Costume Design by Mari Taylor
Lighting Design by Elaine Wong
Sound Design by Janet Bentley
Prop Design by Sarah George
Stage Management by Alannah O'Hagan
Assistant Stage Management by Elizabeth Weber
Line Producer Samuel-James DeMattio
Assistant Director Arthur Ross
Technical Direction by TJ Craftsman

Cast:
TOMMY ....Will Sarratt
ANNE...........................Marcia DeBonis
DAVE ....Xavier Rodney
ALICE......................... Lisa Jill Anderson

PHOTO CREDITS: Hunter Canning

ORIGINAL PRODUCTION BILLINGS (CONT'D)

FLORIDA PRODUCTION

Everything Is Super Great (a comedy about what's missing) opened at Theatre Lab, the professional resident company of FAU, (Matt Stabile, Producing Artistic Director; Louis Tyrrell, Founding Director; Desmond Gallant, Associate Producer; Cassandra Kris, Company Manager) on November 30, 2019. The set design was by Michael McClain; the costume design was by Dawn C. Shamburger; the lighting design was by Jayson Tomasheski; the video design was by Nicholas Chimienti; the sound design was by Matt Corey; the properties design was by John Shamburger; the production manager was Michael McClain; and the production stage manager was Rose Figueroa. The cast was as follows:

Cast:

TOMMY .... Christian Mouisset
ANNE .... Jeni Hacker
ALICE .... Rachel Michelle Bryant
DAVE .... Timothy Mark Davis

Theatre Lab, the professional resident company of FAU
Opening: November 30, 2019

Creative & Production Team:
Producing Artistic Director: Matt Stabile
Founding Director: Louis Tyrrell
Associate Producer & Chair of Department of Theatre & Dance:
Desmond Gallant
Company Manager: Cassandra Kris
Production Manager: Michael McClain

Director: Matt Stabile
Stage Manager: Rose Figueroa
Scenic Design: Michael McClain
Lighting Design: Jayson Tomasheski
Costume & Makeup Design: Dawn C. Shamburger
Video Design: Nicholas Chimienti
Sound Design: Matt Corey
Props Master: John Shamburger

PHOTO CREDITS: Julia Rose Photography

EVERYTHING IS SUPER GREAT

CHARACER DESCRIPTIONS

Minimum Casting Requirements: 2F, 2M

TOMMY: 19. Male. A youthful computer nerd who's in love with his assistant manager at Starbucks and close with his mom.

ANNE: 40s-50s. Female. Sweet and sarcastic and lonely. Her children are her world and she'd do anything for them, which sometimes means she steps clear over their boundaries.

ALICE: 21. Female. Extremely overworked and exhausted all the time. She has no patience to sugarcoat or be nice about anything.

DAVE: Mid-late 30s. Male. Has crippling self-esteem issues, but always tries to make the best out of every situation and put a smile on his face. Is bad at most things.

SETTING

Small Town Texas (but no one has an accent). The present.

SET

Since there are so many locations, it's easiest to use an abstract set with one piece of furniture to signal a different place.

APPROXIMATE RUN TIME

The run time is about 100 minutes. However, there's an optional intermission that can happen after Scene 8 (the Florida production did it), and with a 10 minute intermission the production will run about 110 minutes.

SCENE 1

TOMMY'S BEDROOM

TOMMY, 19, is making a video on his laptop.

TOMMY: Hey. Is this— crap, sorry. Hold on—

He fiddles with his computer camera.

–yeah. Okay. Yeah. Hey. Hey! What Uuuuuppp?

He fake laughs like it's funny, but it doesn't work.

Or— yeah. What's up? Sorry I haven't sent you anything in a bit. Things here have been sort of... *intense.* I think last time I updated Applebees had just had their "grand opening" or whatever? And after I posted I went to work and... well mom and this lawyer said I can't talk about it 'cause of, like, "further incriminating myself"? But... I'm not really allowed inside of an Applebees ever again... and I'm gonna have to take these online classes... so, but that's why I haven't—

ANNE (*beyond the door*): Tommy?

TOMMY: What?

ANNE (*offstage*): What are you doing?

TOMMY: Nothing. I'm on the computer.

ANNE (*offstage*): Are you okay?

TOMMY: Yes. What? Yes. Mom, / I'm on the—

ANNE (*offstage*): Are you talking to your diary?

TOMMY: It's not a diary, oh my God—

ANNE (*offstage*): Hey. I need / to talk—

TOMMY: Stop listening outside my door.

ANNE (*offstage*): Okay. I need to talk to you.

TOMMY: Well, can it just— I gotta finish this in like five minutes. Send me an e-mail or something.

ANNE (*offstage*): I did. You never responded.

TOMMY (*sighs*): Fine. I'll— fine. I'll check it later. Alright?

ANNE (*offstage*): Because I did a bunch of research and found this great therapist / in the area—

TOMMY: Okay. Awesome. Okay.

ANNE (*offstage*): And if you want, we could reach out to him / now so that—

TOMMY (*talking over her*): Okay! Awesome! Okay! I'll do it later!

Pause. He listens for her. She's no longer there. Relief.

TOMMY (CONT'D): Sorry. That was all... mom. She's still at Walmart. Which I'm sure you're thrilled about. But um... everything else here is good though! Oh, I was gonna say, DON'T play the new Star Wars game yet. I haven't played it yet and I don't want you ruining it. I'm probably gonna go by Game Stop later today, so don't say / anything before—

ANNE (*offstage*): Do you want me to drive you?

TOMMY: Oh my God!

ANNE (*offstage*): I wasn't listening, / I wasn't.

TOMMY: Mom!

ANNE (*offstage*): I just came back to see if you were hungry?

TOMMY: No.

ANNE (*offstage*): I'm going to make you some pop-tarts.

TOMMY: I'm not hungry.

ANNE (*offstage*): They're Christmas-themed.

TOMMY: Okay. I don't care.

ANNE (*offstage*): How many do you want?

TOMMY: No. That's not— mom. I'm not hungry.

ANNE (*offstage*): Well I just bought you two new boxes of pop-tarts you said you liked and if no one's going to eat them then I guess they're gonna go to waste in which case I don't / know why I buy anything if—

TOMMY: Wow. Wow. Fine. I'll have a pop-tart.

ANNE (*offstage*): Good...

        (Pause)

...did you happen to read my e-mail while / you were—

TOMMY: Please-mom-we'll-talk-about-it-later-please-oh-my-God.

        Pause. She's gone. He looks back to his computer.

Sorry... Um. I guess there's not really that much to update. Um... yeah. Hope you're well. And uh... write back. If you feel like it. So... cool. Signing off.

        He closes his laptop.

SCENE 2

THE STARBUCKS BREAK ROOM

ALICE is doing something on the computer, her massive Starbucks cup by her side. TOMMY enters and sits. They sit there in silence for a long time, Tommy periodically looking over at her. Alice hasn't even glanced at him.

TOMMY: Hey.

ALICE (*not looking up*): Hi.

> *Short pause.*

TOMMY: Yeah. Your break room's pretty cool. All nice and like... white and stuff.

ALICE (*still not looking up*): It reminds me of the mental institution they stuffed my mom in.

> *Short pause.*

Still glad we hired you?

TOMMY: Of course. I love it! Like... I love it.

ALICE: Really?

TOMMY: Yeah! Um. Although. Can I maybe train with someone else this weekend though?

ALICE: You don't like training with Edzo?

TOMMY: No, it's not— I love Edzo. Big fan. And... I just, I know what you're thinking. It's not that.

ALICE: It's not what?

TOMMY: You know... it's not like a race thing.

ALICE: A race thing?

TOMMY: Yeah, like... Taiwanese people and everything.

ALICE: Edzo's Hawaiian.

TOMMY: Yeah. And... he's hardworking. And...

> *(Pause)*

Okay. I can't understand a word he says. Which like... he's the one calling out all the drinks. So... I mean like, what's a Benny Skimp LaDay?

ALICE: Venti skim latte.

TOMMY: Then what's a, it's like a... Demon Gang Crappy?

ALICE: Decaf grande cappuccino.

TOMMY (*dread*): ...so all those were supposed to be decaf...

ALICE: I'm the only trainer working this weekend.

TOMMY: Okay great! Cool. Yeah that's great... cool.

ALICE: ...O-kay. Guess I'll see you this weekend.

TOMMY: Guess so! And I promise I won't suck as much as I do now. I think I'm starting to get it all down. Got it all memorized. Like, like— okay, like what are you drinking?

ALICE: Extra-hot venti skim quad latte.

TOMMY: Right. So... Venti: biggest cup. Extra hot: *really really* hot. Skim: skim milk. And quad latte: two shots.

ALICE: Four shots.

TOMMY: That has four shots in it?

ALICE: Actually it's five today.

TOMMY: Whoa... are you okay?

ALICE: I don't sleep.

TOMMY: Yeah. You've always got these huge circles under your eyes.

ALICE: Thank you...

TOMMY: I mean, they're not like, noticeable, or... they look really good.

> *She goes back to writing. He stares at her.*

Yeeeeah.

ALICE: What?

TOMMY: Nothing. Just, yeah, like "yeeeeah." Or— hey do you like music?

ALICE: No.

TOMMY: Do you like rap?

ALICE: Okay, kid?

TOMMY: 'Cause there's this song? By Lil' Wayne? I think you would totally dig it. It starts out all like— it's a trumpet— it goes

> *He starts singing the instrumental to the rap song. He's into it.*

And then the background vocals jump in and it's like, "What!— What!— What!— What!— What!— What!— What!— What!— What!— What!— What!— What! Oh okay. I got this chrome on this Bugatti. / I'm strong in this Bugatti—

ALICE: Hey kid. Kid!

TOMMY: What?

ALICE: Go make the backups for the mocha.

TOMMY: Oh... okay.

> *He gets up, but doesn't quite move. Stands there.*

ALICE: ...What?

TOMMY: I don't know how to make the backups.

ALICE: Make Edzo show you.

TOMMY: ...Okay.

> *TOMMY walks out. Probably awkwardly. With a hint of longing. Blackout.*

SCENE 3

ANNE AND TOMMY IN THE CAR

Something Christmas-y is playing on the radio. ANNE is driving while putting on her make-up in the rearview mirror. She drives. She looks over at her son. She drives. She looks over at her son again. Staring at him. She reaches out and touches his face.

TOMMY: Whoa! What are you doing?

ANNE: What?

TOMMY: You just groped my face.

ANNE: Well I am so sorry. I guess I won't ever touch you ever again for the rest of my life.

> *(Short pause)*

Did you read those emails I sent you?

TOMMY: Yes.

ANNE: No you didn't.

TOMMY: Why did you ask / then?

ANNE: Okay, listen, 'cause here's the deal. I was looking on the internet last week, right? And I found this great therapist in the area. He's great. Dr. David Allen? And so— well, I've been talking to him and I think you'd really like him. He's pretty young. His patients love him. Um. He's a male. So... I don't know if you care about that part, but— he just seems really cool, you know? Like he seems like the kind of person, like after a session y'all might hang out or do something fun, you know? Something *cool.* So... but of course I want it to be your decision.

TOMMY: No.

ANNE: What?

TOMMY: No. I looked it up. They have these therapy things you can do online.

> *ANNE frowns. Short pause.*

ANNE: I don't know if I like that.

TOMMY: It's interactive, it's fine.

ANNE: I don't know if I like you talking to your computer like that.

TOMMY: Well. That's what I'm doing.

ANNE: No, you need to talk to a person, okay? I mean, I don't think you understand what's going on here—

TOMMY: Mom—

ANNE: No listen, okay? I was watching this news show recently about this boy in New Mexico? Grew up being real sweet, well behaved, B average in school and everything? Right? Real sweet boy.

ANNE (CONT'D): But then one day he started making bad life choices and getting in trouble because *he stopped listening to his mother.* And then pow! Before she knew it, that sweet boy was going to prison for selling meth behind a Hobby Lobby.

> *Beat.*

TOMMY: *What?*

ANNE: In New Mexico. That really happened.

TOMMY: What does that have to do / with anything?

ANNE: I don't want you talking to your computer, you need to talk with someone face-to-face. And not one of those group therapy places either, I heard a woman got stabbed at one of those things.

TOMMY: Mom—

ANNE: And Dr. Allen's different. People really respond to him. You should read the testimonials on his website.

TOMMY: Yeah. And how expensive is he?

ANNE: No. I know him a little bit. It's okay.

TOMMY: Oh God. This isn't like one of your spiritual friends again, / is it?

ANNE: No no— and I told him about our, situation. So.

TOMMY: What did you say?

ANNE: He just— he's happy to give us a discount is all.

TOMMY: Oh my God. I'm doing the online classes.

ANNE: No, I don't think so.

TOMMY: Yeah I am.

ANNE: Okay, well I know that's what you think hon, but you're not.

TOMMY: Really, why not?

ANNE: Because I already hired Dr. Allen.

> *Beat.*

TOMMY: What!

ANNE: Sorry.

TOMMY: You just said it was my decision.

ANNE: I know and I lied to you sweetheart.

> *Off his astonished look:*

But it's gonna be great! Dr. Allen seems very eager to start. I already set up y'all's first session, and—

TOMMY: Well I don't know who he's gonna meet with.

ANNE: Um. It better be you.

TOMMY: We'll see.

ANNE: We will see. You want me to go back to that judge, have her charge you with a felony?

TOMMY: Fine. I love felonies.

ANNE: Oh you love felonies now.

TOMMY: I love 'em!

ANNE: You love felonies.

TOMMY: I wish I had more felonies!

ANNE: Oh! Well! I did not know that!

TOMMY: I know, it's crazy!

ANNE: I guess I should just call up the judge and have her change the sentence!

TOMMY: Do it!

ANNE: I guess I was wrong this whole time!

TOMMY: I guess so!

ANNE: I guess you really do want to get away from me that badly, huh?

TOMMY: Yeah, I do!

Beat. That stung a bit. They drive in silence.

ANNE: I know you think this whole thing is funny. But I'm sure Chazz or whatever the hell his name is over at Applebees'd be perfectly happy trying to get you the full sentence... is that what you want?

He doesn't answer. She's frustrated by this.

She stops the car. They're here. Short pause.

What time should I pick you up?

TOMMY: Three.

ANNE: Well I get off at four, so you should walk over and hang out for a little while.

He looks at her.

TOMMY: Wait, look at me?

ANNE: What?

He licks his finger and rubs off part of her eyebrow.

ANNE (*recoiling*): Ah, what are you doing?

TOMMY: You drew on your eyebrows real weird.

ANNE: No I didn't.

He tries again.

Stop it ya weirdo!

TOMMY: You drew them as perfect triangles.

ANNE: No I didn't, I just touched them up a little. Just on the ends. To give my face a little lift. Ted said I looked depressed all the time.

TOMMY: Well now you look perpetually surprised.

ANNE: Well, *sometimes* we have to do things we don't want to because they're good for us and it'll help heal us and make us into better, healthier people. And because we lost all the hair from our eyebrows.

TOMMY: Whatever. You look way better without them.

> *He gets out of the car and closes the door. ANNE sits alone, watching him go. Pause. Then she looks in the rear-view mirror and wipes off a little make-up.*

SCENE 4

THE OFFICE OF DR. DAVE ALLEN

It's very minimalistic. There's just two comfy chairs with a small table in between them.

DAVE, mid 30-ish is tightening up the space.

He lays out a little plastic thing of muffins on the table. Does that look okay?

He opens the lid to make it look more inviting.

It doesn't really look that inviting.

He closes the box, then opens it again with a flourish, like "heeey, muffins!"

...

No, that's stupid. Just keep it open.

What time is it?

He's like ten minutes late.

What if he doesn't come?

...

...

...

DAVE eats a muffin.

There's a knock at the door. Shit.

Chew chew chew chew chew.

DAVE (*mouth full*): Come in!

TOMMY: Hey...

DAVE: Hi! Tommy?

TOMMY: Are you Dr. Allen?

DAVE: Yeah! Dave. You can just call me Dave.

TOMMY: Okay... Dave.

DAVE: Come in, come in.

>   *TOMMY sits in one of the chairs.*

TOMMY: Sorry I'm late.

DAVE: Oh it's okay!

TOMMY: I got a little lost in the whole, uh...

>   *Vague hand gesture.*

DAVE: Yeah, there's a lot of offices out here. It's a big building.

TOMMY: Yeah.

DAVE: You want a muffin or a water or anything?

TOMMY: I'll take a water.

> *DAVE hands him a water from the side table.*

Thanks.

DAVE: So! How's it going? How are you? Your mom has said such wonderful things about you.

TOMMY: What things?

DAVE: Oh just things... I mean the Applebees, uh, incident, uh... so that's one thing— but also! That you got into UT. Which is great. And that you're excellent with computers. And the internet. And lots of internet things.

TOMMY: "Internet things."

DAVE: Yeah.

TOMMY: Okay.

DAVE: You know, moms can be proud even if they don't know what they're proud of.

TOMMY: Oh, actually she— this is weird. But she wanted me to give you these.

> *He reaches in his backpack and gives DAVE a Tupperware box. Dave opens it.*

DAVE: Whoa... pop-tarts. Okay.

TOMMY: Sorry. It's like the only thing she can make. She just kind of... gives them to everyone.

DAVE: Haha yeah, she used to do this sort of thing all the time.

TOMMY: What do you mean?

DAVE: Always dropping off little snacks and things to people in the break room.

TOMMY: You know my mom?

DAVE: From when we worked together.

TOMMY: You used to work at Wal-Mart?

DAVE: Yeah, she helped me get promoted into the electronics section. It was awesome.

> *TOMMY suddenly looks very skeptical. DAVE pulls out a Walgreens type plastic bag.*

So! Before we jump into this I just wanted to say, I'm really excited about this whole thing. I remember when your mom asked me about doing this I was like, "yes." You know? I was like, "Yes, I will do this." Because she told me what was going on and...

> *(emotional pause)*

...I get it. You know? I get it.

TOMMY: Okay...?

DAVE: Anyway! To kick things off, I thought we'd start with an easy like get-to-know-you exercise.

> *DAVE upturns the bag and dumps a bunch of colored pencils and markers and shit on the table.*

DAVE: So we got a bunch of markers and pencils and colored markers here.

TOMMY: What?

DAVE: And I don't know what kind of paper you're partial to, but we have notebook and construction.

TOMMY: Wait... what are we doing?

DAVE: So this is an activity called "Intuitive Drawing." It's a great exercise to just get a sense of where someone is emotionally? And it's really easy! You basically just draw. You draw anything you want. It's supposed to be like how you'd doodle around in class, you know? Like when you were in class and you weren't paying attention and you're drawing on your binder and it was just instinct? I think it'll be a really good jumping off point for us in terms of what we'll be discussing and working through. Okay? But I was thinking we could take like fifteen minutes or so? And once you're done we can talk about it and I'll be able to discuss how the rest of this is going to go. But don't think too much about it. Just like draw. Just go for it. And have fun. It's okay to have fun. I'm talking too much, right? Sorry, I'm talking too much. Anyway! Go ahead? Jump in? No pressure? Go for it? Have fun? And-again-no-pressure! And-again-have-fun... Any questions?

TOMMY: Are you a real therapist?

DAVE (*thinks it's a joke*): Ha. Yeah.

> *(Short pause)*

Oh. You're— are you really asking me?

TOMMY: 'Cause like... where's your desk? Or your receptionist? You don't have a receptionist.

DAVE: It's a new office, we're still moving in here. Ha.

TOMMY: Or like a diploma on your wall. Are you an actual doctor?

DAVE: Yeah, of course. I mean not, *technically*, no. But yeah.

TOMMY: What?

DAVE: I have an MFA.

TOMMY: They give out MFA's in anger management?

DAVE: Sort of. It's a cool little hybrid form I created at school called "Anger Management Through the Arts."

TOMMY: Through the *what*?

DAVE: It's sort of like Art Therapy?

TOMMY: Wait, are you one of those guys who tries to cure people by making them paint stuff?

DAVE: Uhhhh— I mean not exactly.

TOMMY: What is it exactly?

DAVE: We also sculpt and create collages.

TOMMY (*with dread*): Oh God.

DAVE: So your mom didn't... tell you that part of it, huh?

TOMMY (*more dread*): Oh my God.

DAVE: It's actually very therapeutic. Intuitive drawing helps you get back to the freedom of art you once knew as a kid.

TOMMY: What does that even mean?

DAVE: And so— hey, maybe if I showed you an example. Here, this is my journal where I do some doodling sometimes, it's just supposed to give you a snapshot of where you are emotionally. It's really good to do in the mornings that way you don't really think about it. Then at the end of the week you can look back at what you've been doing and it really helps / to—

TOMMY: Why did you draw a black hole three days in a row?

DAVE: Uh— so I'm not sure I'd say that's a black hole exactly, but that's okay. If you keep going though it / you'll find that—

TOMMY: This page is just the color red.

DAVE: OKAY so you get the idea. Why don't you take some time and try it out yourself? Here's some paper. A crayon. Why don't you take like 10 minutes and just draw whatever comes out.

TOMMY: ...What if nothing comes out?

DAVE: Good question! Yeah. So part of the exercise is about tapping into any strong feelings you have going on inside. So. I guess... is there anything you feel like you're dealing with right now?

TOMMY: No.

DAVE: Are youuuuuu sure?

TOMMY: Pretty sure yeah.

DAVE: You can talk to me, you know. Or you can always draw it out.

TOMMY: Dude, I'm sure.

DAVE: What about uh... you know. What about your brother?

TOMMY: ...What about him?

DAVE: Well, I don't have experience with this personally, but I'm sure having your older brother go missing would have a significant impact on someone.

TOMMY: My brother's not missing.

DAVE: What!

TOMMY: What?

DAVE (*alarm*)**:** Uhhhh.

TOMMY: Oh my God, did my mom tell you that?!

DAVE: She told me...

TOMMY: Oh my God.

DAVE: So he's... not?

TOMMY: Oh my *God.*

DAVE: Aw shit. I messed that up.

TOMMY: This is just / like...!

DAVE: I shouldn't have brought that up.

TOMMY: She *always* does this!

DAVE: No it's not her / fault it's my fault—

TOMMY: Always saying shit that's like—

DAVE: I wasn't supposed / to bring that up until later.

TOMMY: What else / did she say?

DAVE: No, this is / on me—

TOMMY: What?

DAVE: --God COME ON, Dave!

TOMMY: Whoa.

DAVE: You *ruined* it!

TOMMY: Hey. / It's okay—

DAVE: Get it together!

> He slams a muffin on the table and crushes it. Super
> awkward pause.

TOMMY: Dude... you just destroyed that muffin.

DAVE: Yeah. I'm really sorry. I'm not uh...

TOMMY: You want some water?

DAVE: No.

TOMMY: You should have some water.

DAVE: Okay.

> TOMMY hands DAVE the bottle of water.
>
> DAVE takes it and drinks.

TOMMY: Yeah, there you go.

> Gulp.
>
> Gulp.

> *Gulp.*
>
> *Gulp... gulp... ...gulp... ... ...gulp... ... ...gulp... ... ...gulp.*
>
> *Gulp.*
>
> *He finishes the whole bottle.*

DAVE: Okay... So *that* was an example of someone not really controlling their emotions. And so now I'm thinking, "Hey Dave, I wonder why you smashed the muffin back there? That was strange." *Good thing* I have my journal with me and can figure it out through the art of drawing. You see? You see how it all connects? It alllll connects. Everything's fine. I'm totally fine right now. So why don't we give this intuitive drawing another shot. Sound good?

TOMMY: Actually? I forgot I switched to an earlier shift at work, so I gotta run earlier. Can you just tell my mom this was an hour?

DAVE: Uh.

TOMMY: Thanks.

> *TOMMY leaves. DAVE stands there, defeated.*

SCENE 5

THE STARBUCKS BREAK ROOM

It's closing time. ALICE is typing on the computer or filling out time sheets. TOMMY comes in already buttoned up in his jacket.

TOMMY: Okay. I unloaded the whipped cream into the bottom fridge for tomorrow, re-packed the sugar containers and took all the trash out to the back.

ALICE: And the recycling?

TOMMY: Yeah and the recycling. It's like 30 degrees outside now. Aw man, you know it might snow next week? That's what my mom said. Wouldn't that be awesome?

ALICE: Why would that awesome?

TOMMY: 'Cause... snow?

> *ALICE stares at him.*

Or— okay! I'm gonna take off then I think... You need anything before I go?

ALICE (*turning back to her work*): No.

TOMMY: Cool. Thanks for the advice, and I think I know the thing about the beans now, but, it...

> *She's not paying attention. He waves goodbye? He doesn't know. He walks out. ALICE sorts whatever files she's working on. Then stops... She listens. She looks out the door, checking the hall. Then she pulls out a small prescription pill bottle filled with a couple blunts and a lighter. This should feel like something of a ritual for her.*

> *Tommy walks back in with a whipped cream bottle.*

TOMMY: Hey so I forgot about this one bottle missing its cap and I...

> *He sees what she's doing.*

...didn't know if you wanted to keep it... But I can just leave it, if you're busy.

ALICE (*sighs, so annoyed*): Do you smoke?

TOMMY: Um...

> (*Lying*)

Yes. Absolutely.

> *She passes him the blunt and lighter. He picks it up like it's a foreign object.*

So do you do this a lot? / Or.

> *She looks at him.*

Or— yeah, we don't have to talk. I'll just...

> *He doesn't know what he's doing. He takes a monster hit accidentally. COUGHS.*

TOMMY (CONT'D): Wow. Okay...

> *(Really feeling the effects)*

Oooookay.

> *ALICE takes a masterful hit. She relishes it.*

> *Long pause as they listen to Michael Buble from the speakers.*

ALICE: I fucking hate Michael Buble.

TOMMY: What?

ALICE: Somebody should fucking kill that guy.

TOMMY: Yeah...

ALICE: I used to work at this guy's Dollar General when I was still at UT? He was German and almost definitely born in the 1800s. We'd get complaints all the time because the only thing he'd play was *intense* classical music. It was great. He'd play that shit on full blast and all the customers would get pissed and leave and I'd be like *"Hell* yeah Vladislav." I went back there to pick up the rest of my shit from school and they had turned his store into a Starbucks. And you know what they were playing? The same God damn Michael Buble album we are.

TOMMY: Did you like UT when you were there?

ALICE: ...Why?

TOMMY: No, just 'cause I'm actually going there. Or... I'm *gonna* go there, I'm doing like a gap year thing right now, but I was just gonna say like— that'd be pretty cool to see you at school there. Were you studying the cello?

ALICE: What?

TOMMY: 'Cause didn't you— you used to play the cello, right?

ALICE: Who told you that?

TOMMY: Because you were uh— When they did concerts? At school. You were always in them. Right? My friend Adam Roberts played the violin and I'd have to wait around for him after, so sometimes I'd come in and watch y'all... You used to get all the solos. Right? Um... yeah so I was just curious if that's what you were studying, 'cause like. 'Cause your solos were always really, um... beautiful.

> *ALICE looks at him for a moment. Was she moved by this?*

ALICE: We went to high school together?

TOMMY *(devastated)*: Yes...

ALICE: Really?

TOMMY: And middle. And elementary school.

ALICE: Dude I thought you were like sixteen. What's your name again?

TOMMY (*pointing to name tag*): Tommy. Tommy Fleming...?

ALICE: Wait... you're not like... that *kid* are you?

TOMMY: What?

ALICE: Holy shit are you that kid? That like— that kid that died or went missing or something?

TOMMY: Oh. Um—

ALICE: With all those flyers and posters everywhere?

TOMMY: Right, yeah. Um, no. It / wasn't—

ALICE: Damn. That would've been nuts... I still see those things everywhere. It's so stupid.

TOMMY: What? Why?

ALICE: Um...

> *She laughs.*

...'Cause like, there were hundreds of those things, on like every tree and stop sign and, like our town was one big missing person poster. It's like, post it online. Send an e-mail to everyone. Don't litter the entire neighborhood. The gutter on my street got clogged with those things when we had that flash flood in June. The *gutter*.

TOMMY: ... I don't know. Maybe if you post it on the internet and send it to everyone, no one responds. Maybe the person who made all of them was just trying to like, accommodate for the fact that the newspaper and media coverage on missing persons is totally lopsided and bullshit. It's like, have you ever noticed that only beautiful people go missing? And people treat it like more than a tragedy— like, "Oh, they were so gorgeous or whatever, they had such a bright future, how could this happen?" Obviously less-than-attractive people get kidnapped too, but no one wants to look at them, so nobody in any news department gives a shit. Or if they did drugs like, *once,* then obviously they were involved in some big drug crime ring or something so they deserved it. Or if they're male, they clearly weren't kidnapped, they just ran away and I'm sure they'll show up again, so just wait around while we use zero of our resources to find them. I mean, what the fuck man! Maybe putting posters up is like, *the only thing you can do!*

> *Beat. They sit there. ALICE perplexed. TOMMY embarrassed. He suddenly gets up and crosses the room while punching the air. Then he just as suddenly stops. He breathes.*

ALICE: Um... what was that?

TOMMY: I don't know. Nothing. Sometimes I just have to like, punch it out. You know?

> *No response.*

TOMMY (CONT'D): That's weird. I don't actually do that. Sorry. I've never been high before. Am I high? Sometimes I just have this urge that's like, it's like this heat, and it comes out in weird ways. Like my last job? My boss sucked. And I almost burned the place down. And that was crazy. / And then—

ALICE: Wait, what?

TOMMY: Yeah. I totally lied to you guys in my interview. I never quit Applebees, I almost burned it to the ground.

ALICE: On accident?

TOMMY: ...no.

> *Beat.*

Which I realize sounds bad. But— Okay, so... I had like, a five top of some douchebag father and his family. It was his birthday and they were celebrating. At an Applebee's. So they were ordering and his like, four-year-old son wanted macaroni and cheese, but his dad ordered him a caesar salad because he was like, "Oh you don't want to end up fat like your mother." And the mother, like, nodded her head like she knew?! Anyway, so the kid's like seven year-old brother started slipping him goldfish crackers under the table 'cause obviously he was hungry. And then when the dad found out he made this big show about calling me over and saying like "You can't reward bad behavior," and then making me take away their plates before they even touched it. And it's like, *really man*? You couldn't let 'em eat goldfish crackers? They're kids! Just let them be sneaky! And so when I told my manager. Chad. He was like, "Kids should've eaten their fucken salads." So then I had to set up this guy's *complimentary* birthday cake which he wasn't gonna let his sons eat. And I was lighting the candles. Alone. And then I stopped, and I was like, "You know what dude? Fuck your fucking birthday cake!" And then I slam dunked that shit into the trash can and it caught fire!

> *Long beat.*

...Am I fired?

ALICE: That is so. Fucking. AWESOME.

TOMMY: Really??

ALICE: Yeah!

TOMMY: Yeah? Yeah. Yeah!

ALICE: Then what happened?!

TOMMY: Then the like, the trashcan erupted into flames 'cause I actually threw it into the paper recycling on accident. And then I just sat there, like, watching it burn. You know? Like, like, *gazing into the flame.*

ALICE: *The flame.*

TOMMY: And so I started throwing more shit in it. Like straws, and to-go boxes, and little packets of salt, and like, coffee filters!

ALICE: Yeah you did!

TOMMY: Yeah. I did.

ALICE: Yeah. Open your mouth.

TOMMY: What?

ALICE: *Open your mouth!*

> *He opens his mouth. She sprays whipped cream in it. Then she sprays some in hers.*

Keep going!

TOMMY: And then I got arrested!

ALICE: Did you resist?!

TOMMY: Um— Hell yeah I resisted!

ALICE: Fuck yeah you resisted!

TOMMY: Yeah I like, kicked one of those pigs in the shin and then he pulled his gun on me! That part didn't actually happen, but I did get arrested.

ALICE (*excited*): Did you go to jail?

> *She sprays more whipped cream into his mouth.*

TOMMY: No, but I was charged with a felony!!

ALICE: *What?*

TOMMY: Yeah! But then my mom blasted into the cop station and was like, "It was an accident, he has problems, blah blah blah!" And they made it a misdemeanor.

ALICE: You have problems?

TOMMY: No, no, no. Just like, anger and depression and... other things.

> *ALICE starts laughing. TOMMY hesitantly laughs with her.*

Yeah. Yeah and then I promised my mom I'd go to therapy.

> *Alice laughs even harder.*

And now I have to draw my emotions with a guy named Dave.

> *They're both laughing now.*

ALICE: That's amazing. You're amazing.

TOMMY: ...You're amazing.

ALICE (*still laughing*): I think about killing my mom.

TOMMY (*also laughing*): What?

ALICE: Yeah. I mean, not kill her. But just— like tonight? What if I didn't go home? What if I stopped taking care of her? What would happen? It's so fucked up, right?

TOMMY (*still laughing*): No.

ALICE: No. It is. It's so fucked.

TOMMY: But isn't your mom fine? Isn't she, I don't know, at home? Asleep?

ALICE (*laughing*): No. No. She's probably sitting in the same chair that I left her in this morning, repeating the same three words, and still not having touched any of her oatmeal, so sure, she's most likely lost two or three pounds today.

> *She starts calming down.*

Or, and this is probably more likely, she's bumbling down the middle of our street trying to catch fireflies. And they think she has Alzheimer's, but they're not sure? So my step-dad tried to shove her into a— into this "Sunny Meadows Specialist Center." Which, of course, is a bullshit name for a mental institution. But what does he care, he lives in like a motel room. Which is just— pathetic. Right? God.

> *She tries to laugh at her insult, but it doesn't work. Her smile slowly, slowly sinks. Long pause.*

Sorry.

TOMMY: For what?

ALICE: I don't know.

> *(Pause)*

She used to do theater all the time? At Playhouse 1960? So, not professionally, but she used to play the leads in all the musicals? Well— they were actually plays they added music to— she was in Death of a Salesman as Willy Loman's wife? But she sang a couple songs from South Pacific and the Sound of Music for some reason. It wasn't good. And she knew that, which only made it really fucking fun to watch... Last night I found her wandering in the back yard because she couldn't find the house...

> *Long pause.*

TOMMY: I think it's sort of like Star Wars. Just because they're not mentally or physically there doesn't mean they're gone. Like Obi-won Kenobi. And of course you get pissed off. It's like, what the fuck Obi-wan? You totally bitched out and gave up on Vader. You had him! And then you fucking left... But like, I think just talking to them is important. Even if they can't necessarily hear you. They're still there. In spirit or in memory or, you know, the force.

> *They're very close.*

ALICE (*almost a whisper*): ...Open your mouth.

> *He does. She sprays a tiny amount of whipped cream in his mouth. Then a tiny amount in her mouth. They stare at each other.*

SCENE 6

NIGHTTIME - THE FRONT YARD OF ALICE'S HOUSE

There's a giant, plastic, light-up Santa Claus face hanging on her front door.

ALICE slogs up her yard still in her Starbucks uniform. When she walks up to her door the Santa head blares out a "Meeeeeeerry Christmas!" She doesn't even flinch.

She unlocks her front door and goes in. Long pause... the front door opens abruptly, ALICE looks frantic. She runs down her yard. Santa blares a, "Ho Ho Hooooo." She looks around. Up her street. Up the neighbor's driveway. Nothing. She disappears running down her street.

In the Wal-Mart break room, ANNE sitting in one of the chairs. She has her shoes off, with one foot in her chair, massaging it. With her other hand, she's making a phone call.

DAVE is sitting on his couch. His phone rings.

DAVE: Hello?

ANNE: Hi, David? It's Anne.

DAVE: Hi. Hey! What's going on?

ANNE: Sorry. I didn't think you'd pick up. Is this— are you busy? I was just gonna leave a message or something.

DAVE: No, it's fine. I'm just... sitting here.

ANNE: Me too! I'm just sitting here too. I was just calling 'cause you know, I know you're not supposed to tell me anything, like what y'all talk about, but I just wanted to check in to see how y'all's first session went.

DAVE (*dreading this question*): Uh. It went... great!

ANNE (*actually surprised*): Really?

DAVE: Yeah. I mean, it was sorta like an intro session, so not much ever happens in those, but. Why? What— did he say something?

ANNE: Oh, he never tells me anything. I mean— well he did say it was the worst thing that's ever happened? But he says that about everything.

DAVE (*not sure how to respond*): Good.

ANNE: You shouldn't take anything he says too personally, you know? 'Cause he'll say things like— like he always tells me I don't know anything? Which, you know. I do know things. Right?

DAVE: Right.

ANNE: Or like, he thinks that your office isn't a real office. Which, obviously, I'm sure it is.

DAVE: Well actually. We were in a temporary office yesterday. 'Cause my other office is getting... painted.

ANNE: Oh! Really? What color are y'all painting it?

DAVE: Lllllllllavender.

> *He puts his head in his hand. That's the color you thought of DAVE? Really?*

ANNE: Shut. Up.

DAVE: Okay.

ANNE: I love lavender!

DAVE: Really?

ANNE: It's my all-time favorite color.

DAVE: Oh, cool!

ANNE: It's also the color of my aura. So.

DAVE: Okay. Your— wait, what?

ANNE: Yeah. 'Cause I took this quiz in this book one time? About the kinda auras people have, because of their magnetic energy fields and so forth? And there's tons of 'em. There's blue and green and purple and, and like white-silver auras and things? And so I calculated my quiz and it said my aura is lavender. Which means I'm a nurturing person and I'm real good with most animals.

DAVE: Wow.

ANNE: I can send you the quiz if you want.

DAVE: Yeah. Maybe.

ANNE: Oh— did you get those other things I sent?

DAVE: The pop-tarts! Yeah.

ANNE: Oh good. Good. You just looked a little malnourished last time I saw you is all. And that's not an insult, 'cause you don't look bad. You look fine. You look really great. It's just malnourished. Like a little deer.

DAVE: Well, thank you. They were really delicious.

ANNE: You don't have to do that. It was real easy. You know, just pop 'em in the microwave and all.

DAVE: Well. Awesome job, doing that.

ANNE (*like it's a secret*): Of course, the box says to toast them at the lowest setting for one heating cycle? But that's not right. I like to put some butter on them and microwave 'em for 48 seconds on the second setting? That way the butter gets to seep into it, you know?

DAVE: Wow. You're like a chef.

ANNE (*blushing*): Nooo.

DAVE: Seriously. You could like, you could be on that show!

ANNE: Stop, which show?

DAVE: Iron Chef.

ANNE (*blushing more*): No, shut up.

DAVE: "Iron Anne," right? I mean, I don't know how the show works, but.

ANNE: Hey you know what? If your office isn't ready, you could always come over and do your sessions over here at our apartment.

DAVE: No, that's— thank you. I don't want to intrude on / your—

ANNE: No, you wouldn't be. 'Cause that way y'all won't have to worry about, you know, dealing with people coming and going and you could get stuff from the fridge if you want. And maybe I could like sit in on one of y'all's sessions or something.

DAVE: Oh. Uh...

ANNE: Or— maybe not sit in, but. 'Cause I remember you telling me about all the kinds of things you do, and— I'd just love to see that. You know? I'd love to even do one of them... is that weird? Sorry. That's weird.

DAVE: No, no.

ANNE: I just want to be able to talk to Tommy about it, you know? 'Cause like, when his brother would do something— his brother liked to paint? And when his brother would paint something, I'd try to be like, "That looks so good, honey." And he'd be like, "It's not supposed to look good!" And I'd be like, "Ooohhh, okay." And then he wouldn't talk to me for a week. And I always thought things would work themselves out between us, but then... and now I just see that same thing with Tommy, you know? I mean he's supposed to go off to school this year but he's not. He's just, like at work or in his room. Alone. All day. Alone. Talking to his computer. And I'm like, I'm not a computer but I can talk. You know? I can talk a lot. I can talk as much as you want me to— I can talk for days! So...

> *Slight pause.*

DAVE: Yeah—

ANNE: Anyway. Sorry. I just wanted to / call and—

DAVE: Yeah. Well— you know what, how about I send you a list of the kinds of things we're going to be doing and if you want you can take a look and we'll do one of them.

ANNE: Yeah?

DAVE: Sure. Of course.

ANNE: Okay, well... good then. I'll look forward to it. And hey. Seriously. Think about doing y'all's sessions over here, if you want. I know Tommy would really like it...

DAVE: Yeah. I'll think about it.

ANNE: Okay... night!

DAVE and ANNE hang up. She looks at her phone and smiles.

After a moment, ALICE returns to her door, completely out of breath. She stands there for a moment looking at her house, then around the neighborhood for something, anything... Then quietly walks up her front yard into her house. And closes the door.

"Meeeeerry Christmas."

SCENE 7

THE FRONT YARD OF ALICE'S HOUSE

TOMMY enters in his Starbucks uniform holding a stack of posters. He knocks on her door. ALICE opens it. She looks awful.

TOMMY: Hey!

ALICE: How do you know where I live?

TOMMY: Uhhhhh and... so anyway, I saw you weren't at work, and I was like, "Ah geez— that sucks." And then I was like, "Oh man, I wonder what happened to her!" Like maybe something crazy, or like... awful. Right?

ALICE: I called out this morning.

TOMMY: Yeah. I heard.

ALICE: Did you leave in the middle of a shift?

TOMMY: I'm on my lunch break.

ALICE: You need to go back to work.

TOMMY: I know but I just wanted to see if you needed anything.

ALICE *(closing the door)*: ...Thanks. I'm fine.

TOMMY: —Or if you wanted help looking for her.

> *(Beat)*

Um, I just— I know a little bit about this... *situation*? You're in right now? There's just like, certain patterns and tell-tale signs to judge abductions from runaways— specific personality traits that add into the equation— where you might find them / and—

ALICE: How do you know?

TOMMY: I probably shouldn't— can't say.

ALICE: How do you know!

TOMMY: Edzo told me.

> *ALICE looks down like, "Fucking Edzo."*

But anyway, it's been like 35 hours or something since she... which is like, this is the moment. This is that important span of time, so I don't know if you want help or like... if you were still looking?

ALICE: What's that supposed to mean?

TOMMY: No, nothing. It's just— I mean you're at home, so—

ALICE: What do you think I was doing all last night and this— why do you think I'm not at work?

TOMMY: That's not— no! / That's not what I—

ALICE: I haven't slept in 30 hours. Of course I'm still looking.

TOMMY: I didn't know if you'd found her, or— that's all I meant. I didn't know the *update.*

ALICE: Do you see her here?

TOMMY: ...No.

ALICE: Okay then.

TOMMY: Okay...Sorry. I— sorry.

ALICE looks down at the posters in TOMMY's hand.

ALICE: What are those?

TOMMY: Oh— OH! I totally forgot. So, I used the computer to make these.

He shows them to ALICE.

So, they're not great? I just, I had to make them like, real fast. And also, the picture kind of— I found it on your facebook page (sorry about that) and I had to enlarge it by like 800% is why it's so pixelated.

ALICE: Oh my God.

TOMMY: What?

ALICE: No. This isn't— no. Why did you make these?

TOMMY: I thought it would help?

ALICE: Did people see these walking here?

TOMMY: No, but—

ALICE: Did the people at work see these?

TOMMY: No.

ALICE: Are you sure?

TOMMY: Yeah.

She breathes.

But I stapled them to like thirty trees on the way over here.

ALICE: *What?* Why'd you do that? Why'd you— who asked you to do that?

TOMMY: I was trying to help.

ALICE: By putting up your stupid flyers?

TOMMY: ...Yeah?

ALICE: They need to come down.

TOMMY: No, but— You have to do this.

ALICE: I really don't.

TOMMY: No one even knows she's missing!

ALICE: This is a family matter. Since you're not in my family, you don't need to be concerned.

TOMMY: No, *think* for a second! It sounds like your mom accidentally wandered off, right? So if people see her they're just gonna think, "Hey, there's some woman taking a walk" or whatever, they're not gonna think she's lost *unless* they see something like this. You know? Don't just like... leave her out there.

> *Beat.*

ALICE: You need to go back to work.

TOMMY: I don't wanna go back to work.

ALICE: Then go home.

TOMMY: I don't wanna go back there either.

ALICE: Then choose something else. But please get off my lawn.

> *ALICE slams the door shut. The Santa Claus face rips off a: "Meeeerry Christmas." TOMMY sulks away.*

SCENE 8

TOMMY'S BEDROOM

DAVE is in the middle of blowing up a balloon for an exercise they're doing. TOMMY looks to be in a state of utter confusion and apathy. When done, Dave ceremoniously hands the balloon to Tommy.

DAVE: "I bequeath our anger to you."

TOMMY: ...What?

DAVE: I— I bequeath, our / anger—

TOMMY: What are we doing?

DAVE: Okay. So. This is a fun little stress relief exercise called "floating away your anger." Where, what we're gonna do, is blow all of our bad thoughts and anger into an ordinary balloon. And then we're gonna set it free. And by doing this (*with weight?*) we're actually setting your anger free.

TOMMY: Okay. Dude? Today is not the day for the balloon exercise.

DAVE: Now after you blow it up you're gonna want to give your balloon a name. And this is pretty important. Don't name it just anything. Think about where that anger, where that rage in your balloon comes from. So, for instance, let's call this one Rachel.

TOMMY: Who's Rachel?

DAVE: She's just, a— an example name.

TOMMY: Then can we call this one Chad?

DAVE: We're gonna call it Rachel. So you want to write the name on it.

> *Dave writes "Rachel" on his balloon with a sharpie.*

And *then* we're gonna release it. And this is an important part, because you'll want to release it with a word or a phrase or something that really lets you let it go, like "Fly!" or "I release you!" or "Why did you do that to me?!!" and then you release it!

> *DAVE releases the balloon and it flutters slowly to the ground.*

TOMMY: Shouldn't we have helium for this?

DAVE: And I'm realizing now that yes we should have helium but you know what? The past is the past, so! We're gonna do this as a joint exercise. I'll blow them up, and you can write the name. Okay? So:

> *(Ceremoniously)*

I bequeath our anger to you.

> *DAVE hands him the balloon and a sharpie marker. Beat. TOMMY hates this. Tommy starts writing. The balloon pops.*

That's cool. That's okay.

> *DAVE blows up another balloon. He ties it.*

DAVE (CONT'D): I bequeath our anger to you.

> *He hands him the balloon. TOMMY writes. It pops.*

Okay. That's fine. That's fine. Maybe a little gentler. But that's fine.

> *DAVE blows up another balloon. He ties it.*

I bequeath our anger to you.

> *He hands him the balloon. It pops immediately.*

TOMMY: Where did you get these balloons?

DAVE: Ha.

> *DAVE blows up another balloon.*

I bequeath our anger to you.

> *He hands it to him. It pops. But DAVE is already blowing up another balloon.*

I bequeath our anger to you.

> *It pops.*

I bequeath our anger to you!

> *It pops.*

I-bequeth-our-anger-to-you!

> *It pops.*

I bequeath all of our anger to you!

> *It pops!*

I bequeath our anger to you!!!

> *It pops!*

COME ON, MAN!

TOMMY: I'm trying!

DAVE: Really?!

TOMMY: Probably.

DAVE: Okay. Dude?

TOMMY: Are you sure you've done this before?

DAVE: Why don't we start over.

TOMMY: 'Cause it kind of seems like you've never done this before.

> *DAVE starts blowing up another balloon.*

Also I was looking at your website earlier and I'm pretty sure none of your old patients are real people.

> *DAVE stops mid-blow. He slowly lets the air out and turns.*

DAVE: ...What?

TOMMY: Your old patients on your testimonials page? Liz Palmer and that Jonathan Wu and Warren Adams?

DAVE: What about them?

TOMMY: I found all of their pictures under Google Stock Images.

> *Beat.*

Like, Liz Palmer is also known as "young caucasian woman sitting on beach" and Jonathan is actually "Asian kid with computer."

> *(Short pause)*

...Wait... oh my God. Am I like, your first patient?

> *Tiny beat.*

DAVE: Okay here's the thing.

TOMMY: Oh my god!

DAVE: It's not my fault! I / had to put—

TOMMY: Are you even a real therapist?

DAVE: Yes I'm certified! I'm / totally certified! But—

TOMMY: Is your name even Dave?

DAVE: But I had a lot of trouble getting / started after I graduated?

TOMMY: Isn't lying like this against the law or / something?

DAVE: Look-it's-really-hard-finding-work-as-an-art-therapist-especially-when-you-have-an-anxiety-disorder-and-your-only-work-experience-is-at-Walmart-and-then-your-girlfriend-who-you-love- more-than-like-anything-ever-leaves-one-day-and-you-have-no-idea-where-she-went-and-you-really- miss-her-and-I'm-trying-to-get-her-to-come-back-but-like everything's been terrible for a long time now and I just feel super lost pretty much every day.

> *Pause.*

TOMMY: What?

DAVE: I went through a hard time. People go through hard times. But I rose back up? Because that's what people do? Sometimes? And so yes I may have gotten my friend to create a website and lied to your mom about it? And I spent like $500 on an office space that I only used once? And it's not even really used as an office space, it's more of a common area at my friend's workplace? And yes, you are sort of my first patient. And I'm really sorry about that. But you know what? I like you. I like you, man. You're really cool and— I get it, you hate doing this. I know that. But you still show up. You could totally flake on these sessions or just refuse to meet, but you show up. You gotta respect someone who shows up. if you want you can totally go tell your mom and we can stop this whole thing. But I'm here for you, man. I'm here now and I really want to help.

> *Pause.*

TOMMY: You sunk $500 into that office?

DAVE: ...It was actually more like $600.

TOMMY (*laughs*): Oh my God.

DAVE: It wasn't that bad.

TOMMY: It was *so* bad.

DAVE: I know.

TOMMY: You didn't even have your name on the door.

DAVE: Were they really Google stock images?

TOMMY: Yeah.

DAVE: Aw man!

TOMMY: On like, the first page of the search results.

DAVE: Come on Dave!

TOMMY: And wait, what happened to your girlfriend?

DAVE: Oh, that... nothing.

TOMMY: She just left?

DAVE: You know, we don't have to— I sorta revealed a lot of information back there that I probably shouldn't have.

TOMMY: Okay... yeah I mean we can just end the session right now if you want...

Beat.

DAVE: Okay, she didn't actually "leave me" leave me.

TOMMY: What does that mean?

DAVE: She just... took all of her stuff and maybe some of my stuff and moved out and I haven't seen her in like a little while.

TOMMY: What!

DAVE: *But.* Everything's totally fine. Everything's great. She's just showing me some tough love right now.

TOMMY: So wait, where is she now?

DAVE: ...That's a good question.

TOMMY: You don't know? Why don't you just call her?

DAVE: Well she's being real extreme with her tough love thing right now. And I'm pretty sure she changed her phone number.

TOMMY: What about email?

DAVE: Also her email.

TOMMY: When was the last time you saw her?

DAVE: Like three months ago.

TOMMY: What's her name?

DAVE: Rachel.

TOMMY: No, her full name.

DAVE: Rachel Forrester?

>   *TOMMY thinks of something. Goes to the computer.*

TOMMY: Okay, okay, so...

>   *(To himself)*

Email would probably take too long, but...

DAVE: What?

TOMMY: Does she have an account with any subscription-based websites?

DAVE: Yeah, Art Deadline?

TOMMY: What's her username?

DAVE: Uhhhh. She'd never let me use it...

TOMMY: That's okay, that'd be too easy.

DAVE: Wait, what are we doing?

TOMMY (*hesitating*): Uh... so I'm kind of an admin on this forum that sorta helps... find people?

DAVE: Find people?

TOMMY: Yeah. 'Cause like... okay, you know how when people disappear, everyone like automatically thinks the worst? Like, they were abducted or they're in a, you know, someplace bad? Well, that's actually really stupid. 'Cause in reality, a huge percentage of those people are runaways. Like 76% or something.

DAVE: Whoa.

TOMMY: Yeah. And I mean, some are just juveniles who are trying to get out of their foster care situation or whatever? But the rest are just, like... people. Like regular people. Who completely take off from their lives and don't tell their families where they are, what happened, what's going on— which is like...

DAVE: Sucks.

TOMMY: Right?! Like, your people deserve to know where you are. Even if you don't want to talk to them anymore. Like.

DAVE: Yeah, not gonna lie, it would've been great if Rachel had left like... a note.

TOMMY: OH! What about this one?

DAVE (*reading*): "ForestForTheTrees84". She was born in 1984.

TOMMY: Yeeeeahh she was.

DAVE: Why do you need her username?

TOMMY: Well, I don't need it? But it's way easier to just break into her account than insert a backdoor into her email and comb through it. Plus, subscription-based websites usually have their billing info? So I'm running a program that's basically beating the shit out of their network so I can collect their data stream. Then after I bypass their antivirus software I should be able to get her password.

DAVE: Wow...

> *He looks at TOMMY.*

...You're like really impressive.

TOMMY: Shut up.

> *DAVE watches TOMMY work for a second.*

DAVE: And so um... has this forum thing ever um... ever helped you look for your brother?

TOMMY: Yeah. They... tried.

DAVE: Okay.

TOMMY: But like, this is the thing that nobody understands. Is that he's not actually like, "missing" missing.

> *DAVE looks at him.*

'Cause— okay. He took his finals at school back in May? And then like, just because no one heard from him for a while, everyone started to freak out. But just because you don't hear from someone, doesn't mean something awful's happened. Or like, "they were troubled." That's so stupid. Especially 'cause like, my brother is not the type of person who enjoys talking on the phone, texting, anything. Like I email every Monday, just to update him on things and I never get an email back. And that's fine! Because if there was something wrong? Like, really wrong? I would know.

DAVE: What do you mean?

TOMMY: Because he's not like, he's never been someone who talks to other people about his problems. Right? But— so he goes to school about 5 hours away from here, right? So we never see him. But this one time he had this huge falling out with his roommate, I think? And it was a Wednesday. And I was coming out of school to go to the bus. And he just like... showed up, outside my school. He was like, "What's up? Wanna go get Burger King?" I was like, "Sure. Did you just drive four hundred miles?" And he was like "Yeah! Let's do it!" And then we went and got Burger King. And watched two episodes of Battlestar Galactica. And then he drove four hundred miles back to school that night.

> *He types for a moment*

Or like— and this was the worst one. Is he'd been dating this girl for a couple years? And she just like, suddenly broke up with him one day. And the next day I came home from work. And he had driven home from school again. But this time he was like, sleeping in my room on the floor next to my bed...

TOMMY (CONT'D): And when I woke him up, he was just like, "Hey so I'm gonna sleep here for a couple days. Don't tell mom." And so we hung out in my room. For three days. And didn't tell anybody. It was like... it was so awesome...

> *(Short pause)*

...And like, I get it. You know? He just needs to know someone is there. He doesn't need money. Or comfort. He just wants to know that someone is there.

> *He types.*

And it's not like he's even been gone for that long. You know? It's like what, December? Yeah. He's only been gone for like six or seven months. You know? Like, barely six or seven months. So whatever... people can say what they want. But watch. Some night soon. I'm gonna come home from work. And he'll just be sitting there, in my room. And he'll be like, "Hey." And I'll be like, "Hey." And he'll be like, "Wanna go to Burger King?" and I'll be like, "Burger King is terrible." And he'll be like, "Yeahhh let's go." And then we'll hop in the car and go to Burger King.

DAVE: Yeah.

> *Brief pause.*

TOMMY: What do you think you'll say to Rachel when you talk to her?

DAVE: I don't even know.

TOMMY: Well. You should probably figure that out.

DAVE: Why?

TOMMY: Because I JUST FOUND HER PHONE NUMBER!

DAVE: What!

TOMMY: Boom! Rachel Forrester! Right there!

DAVE: You found her?!

TOMMY: I found the shit out of her! She's in

> *(Reading)*

Houston. Her number's 713-303-8840.

DAVE: Why's she in Houston?

TOMMY: You should call her and find out.

DAVE *(suddenly terrified)*: Oh. Uhhhhhh yeah, maybe.

TOMMY: Cool!

> *(Pause)*

Do you want some privacy, or?

DAVE: No, no. That's okay. I'm just— ooohhhh whoa.

> *He bends over like he's going to throw up.*

TOMMY: You okay?

DAVE: Yeah. I don't know. Yeah.

TOMMY: What's wrong?

DAVE: I don't know man. I always imagined I was going to be doing a lot better in life when I finally called her?

TOMMY: Who cares, call her!

DAVE: Oh God she's probably dating like a realtor or something. With fantastic hair. Named like... Rick.

TOMMY: What?

DAVE: Or what if I call and she doesn't even remember me!? What if I call and I'm like, "It's Dave!" and she's like, "Who?" And then I die!

TOMMY: Dude? You have to call her.

DAVE: Aw shit I don't know.

TOMMY: 'Cause if you don't? If you don't call her? You'll regret it forever. This whole "waiting for her thing" will have been for nothing. And you'll move on. And you'll be alone. And years will pass. And you'll forget her face. And you'll get old. And then you'll die alone.

DAVE: Yeah...

TOMMY: And then you'll come back as a ghost. And you'll wander the earth alone. And it'll be like 2147. And you'll have floated around the earth, looking at happy couples, and happy families. And holding out hope for this long and making this one call will seem like the easiest thing you ever could've done.

DAVE: Yeah.

TOMMY: Now you're gonna pick up the phone. Dial her number. And get her back!

DAVE: Yeah. Yeah! Alright, let's do this!

TOMMY throws him his phone. DAVE dials.

HEY!!

(Pause/terror/fear)

What's up? Or— sorry. I know you hate people who say "what's up." Sorry. Um— hey! So. I just wanted to um— call and uh— 'cause I heard you were in Houston! From... somebody. And uh— anyway! I just wanted to call and make sure you were doing okay. And see what's going on in your life. In your new life. 'Cause I hope you're doing well. And— are you um, are you doing any of your installations there? I always really loved those. I probably never said that enough. Especially— oh! The one you did in Austin? "The Seven Lives of Dan"? Yeah. That was sweet. Really really sweet. And, although um— ha— although, I'm not quite sure why all of the "Dan" figures had to be made out of garbage? And also, also, how come you had to exaggerate all of the Dan figures's facial features?

DAVE (CONT'D): 'Cause like, especially after that operation that I got, for you? And how come you had to have that one Dan figure getting ravaged by dogs and have them ripping his trash off? I love dogs! It was really upsetting to have dogs rip Dan's trash off! Maybe Dan shouldn't have been the one made of out trash. Maybe YOU should be the one made out of trash! I DIDN'T MEAN THAT! Ahh! I don't even know what I'm saying anymore! You suck! And I miss you! And every morning I wake up, and I remember who I am, and I remember that you're not there, and it's just... so bad. And also because I'm not even in our bed but my friend Steve's sofa bed. Which sucks even more. Because my back. And everything basically sucks. Alright?!... So call me back if you want!!!

He puts the phone down. He's about to hang up. Then:

This is Dave by the way!

He hangs up. He looks terrible. Pause.

TOMMY: Dude? That was amazing.

Blackout.

SCENE 9

ANNE and DAVE are in the living room. Dave is setting up some art supplies.

ANNE: Did you want anything to drink or anything before we start?

DAVE: Nah, I'm good, thanks.

ANNE: Maybe like a Coke or something? A Diet Coke?

DAVE: I'm okay.

She gets him a Diet Coke.

ANNE: Just in case you change your mind.

DAVE: Thanks.

(Short pause)

So should we start?

ANNE: Oh duh! Sorry, I get distracted.

She goes to kitchen counter and pulls out a manila envelope.

Okay. Hold on. Let me sit down. Sorry. Okay. *Ready.* Go ahead.

DAVE: Which one did you choose?

ANNE: Um, the collage one? Where you like, pick a bunch of things that remind you of someone and it tells you about y'all's relationship? / Or...

DAVE: Yeah, sort of. Essentially, it's a collage that's supposed to revolve around your memories of a single person. You can use pictures, things they've written, basically anything that triggers a memory. It's really easy. But I can help you get started and then after you're done we'll analyze it together. Make sense?

ANNE: Absolutely.

DAVE: Great.

ANNE: Just, if I mess up, you have to tell me, okay?

DAVE: What do you mean, mess up?

ANNE: Like, if I brought the wrong materials or— or like if the stuff I brought isn't creative enough or something.

DAVE: There's not— it's really easy. You can't mess up.

ANNE: Mmmmmmm okay, I don't know if I agree with that.

DAVE: Trust me.

ANNE: Okay, well... we'll see.

She starts pulling things out of her manila envelope.

So, I thought to start with, here are a couple pictures I brought. I don't have that many. I don't know if I lose points for that. So this one's him when he was eight.

DAVE: Whoooaaa, check out Mr. Jedi Knight. Is this Halloween?

ANNE: No. That's just... how he dressed when he was eight. I think that was when those movies came out, so he got all crazy about it.

DAVE: Yeah. He looks like a young Ewan McGregor.

ANNE (*doesn't know who that is*): ...Okay...

> *Another picture.*

And this one's him and Tommy playing "Fireman."

DAVE: "Fireman"?

ANNE: It's one of those games where one of you pretends you're on fire, and then the other one puts you out? So that's him smothering Tommy with the rug... He always made Tommy be the one who was on fire.

DAVE: Who's this?

ANNE: That's them with their dad in front of this church we used to go to.

DAVE: Their dad?

ANNE: Yeah. Jeffrey.

DAVE: And he's...

> *ANNE thinks for a moment.*

ANNE: Somewhere. West Texas. Oklahoma. I stopped keeping track like ten years ago, so.

> *She segues.*

I brought some other things too.

> *(Moving on)*

Like, this is a copy of his acceptance letter to UT. 'Cause we didn't know if that was gonna happen or not and also 'cause he got a full scholarship. And these are some of his debit card statements from last year. Which I usually kept. And this is a clip / from a—

DAVE: His debit card statements?

ANNE: Yeah. Was that— is that wrong?

DAVE: No, no. Just—

ANNE: Shit. I messed it up already, didn't I?

DAVE: No, it's fine. I'm just, curious, why. That's all.

ANNE: Well... so when he went off to college, he started getting real bad about picking up his phone, right? And I mean Tommy's bad too, but. This was like... I mean, after a while it got to where we'd only talk like once... a month? Or... maybe less than that. And it's hard to be able to do things for someone when they won't talk to you, you know? Like, it's hard! So... So but I always got real excited when his debit card statements would come in. 'Cause, see like—

She picks up one of the statements.

ANNE (CONT'D): —okay. This is March? And see how he spent sixteen dollars at Burger King? So I sent him a bunch of BK coupons just in case. And if you look at the week after, he went there like 3 times! And so I was like, "Yes! I did something for him." You know? And so I'd just like use them to like to be on the lookout for things like that.

DAVE: That's so nice.

ANNE: Yeah. But then it sucked, 'cause he stopped sending his statements to the apartment so I had to get Tommy to get me his password so I could check them on the computer, you know. Which was great.

DAVE: Wow.

ANNE: I know.

DAVE (*impressed*): That's like... I think that's like a crime.

ANNE: Yeah...

DAVE: Can I, uh...

ANNE: Oh, sure, sure. I keep all of them. So.

DAVE: What are the highlighted ones?

ANNE: Oh, nothing. Just... those are just some of my favorite entries.

DAVE: What's "El Niño's"?

ANNE: That was a bar near his campus?

DAVE: El Niño's. Nice.

ANNE: I think it's like a Mexican bar or something? He was always sort of like, an introverted kid? You know? And I'd always feel bad that he'd stay in his room and not be going out anywhere with anyone. So, but when I'd see El Nino's come up, I'd be like, "Oh maybe he made some friends" You know? Like, maybe some friends made him go out. And normally he'd only go like once a month. But then all of a sudden he went four times in May. And I was like, "Aaaahhhhhh oh my gosh!!!" So I'd put a little extra money into his account without telling him so he wouldn't worry about going out.

DAVE: Did he ever say anything?

ANNE: About what?

DAVE: I thought you said he wouldn't let you do anything for him.

ANNE: Well, I only ever put a little bit in? Just enough so he wouldn't notice?

DAVE: Mmmmmm I bet he knew.

ANNE: I don't know. Although, he did leave me this one text at like four in the morning after going there that was like, "Hey! I Love Yoouuuuuu!" And I was like, "Oh my God, thank you sweetheart. You just made my day. I love you too!"

DAVE: See.

ANNE: But then he was like, "Oh sorry, that was meant for someone else. Drunk text."

>*(Short pause)*

But, I like to hold on to it anyway... Yeah, May was a real good month for us. I liked May.

DAVE: What about June?

ANNE: Uh. Well... I don't have a statement for June. May 26th is the last purchase I have on here... He spent 3 dollars and 84 cents at a Walgreens... I'm not really sure what you can buy for that much at a Walgreens.

>*(Pause)*

I didn't even find out anything was wrong until the 30th... I hadn't been calling him because he was doing his finals and he hated it when I bothered him like that. So I kept thinking that whole week, I was like, "Ohhh he's gonna be so proud of me for not calling *once* this week. He's gonna be so impressed. Maybe he'll be so impressed he'll let me talk to him for like 10 minutes or something," you know?

>*She laughs at herself and shakes her head.*

I was so excited that whole week.

DAVE: There's nothing wrong with that.

ANNE: You ever find yourself going back and trying to find that, that one mistake you made that made someone not want to talk to you anymore?

DAVE: Yeah. Actually.

ANNE: And do you think... do you think this might be able to tell me that, maybe?

DAVE: What do you mean?

ANNE: 'Cause in your description you said it was supposed to tell you about your relationship with someone, right?

DAVE: Oh. Yeah, but—

ANNE: And like, like things that you wouldn't normally notice or think about. Right?

DAVE: Yeah. But—

ANNE: Well... so do you think maybe this could tell me why he didn't ever want to talk to me?

DAVE: ...It doesn't really work like that.

ANNE: Oh... how does it work?

DAVE: It's more about, analyzing yourself than a relationship.

>*Short pause.*

DAVE (CONT'D): But, you know... If I was to analyze it. Just as it is? I would say that I see someone who cared about her son so much, that she would mail him coupons for things on the off chance that maybe, possibly, he might use them. I see someone who was willing to literally break the law and invade her son's privacy 'cause she wanted to make sure he was eating okay. And yeah, I know this is just a preliminary analysis? But I would say that I see a mom. Who just wanted to do right by her kid.

ANNE (*teary-eyed*): No, shut up.

DAVE: Hey, you could argue with me. Buuuuut I'm the only one here with a masters in this field. So... you kind of have to believe me.

       Blackout.

SCENE 10

THE STARBUCKS BREAK ROOM

It's empty except for Michael Buble's sweet voice bleeding in from the lobby. ALICE comes running in holding her hand. TOMMY stumbles in behind her. It's chaos.

ALICE (*to herself*): Fuck fuck fuck fuck fuck fuck.

TOMMY: Where did you get burned?

ALICE: What?

TOMMY: Let me see it.

ALICE: What are you doing? Get back out there! Edzo's getting slammed!

> *TOMMY gets a look at her hand.*

TOMMY: Oh my God!

> *TOMMY runs out of the room. ALICE sits there, blowing on her hand. It's incredibly red.*

ALICE (*to herself*): Fuck fuck fucking shit fuck idiot— Ow!... Stupid fucking idiot.

> *TOMMY runs back in with a 3-gallon bucket filled with ice.*

TOMMY: Okay! Quick! Dunk your hand.

ALICE: I'm fine.

TOMMY: Do it! It needs to be immersed!

ALICE: I said I'm fine!

> *He grabs her hand.*

What are you doing?! Don't touch me!

TOMMY: Your hand's gonna keep burning unless you dunk it in the bucket! Just / put it in the—

ALICE: Who do you think you are?! I didn't / ask you to—

TOMMY: DUDE!! DUNK YOUR HAND IN THE BUCKET OR I SWEAR TO GOD! PLEASE! I SWEAR TO GOD!

> *She immediately immerses her hand in the ice bucket. The pain is crazy.*

ALICE (*harsh whisper*): Oh my God this sucks this is so awful this is way fucking worse.

TOMMY: I know don't take it out.

ALICE: You don't know how this feels.

TOMMY: I used to work the fryer at Tex Mex Taqueria!

ALICE: What?!

TOMMY: Just, squeeze my hand or something—

> *She grabs his hand. And crushes it. They stay like that a long time. Like 30 seconds to a minute of silence. Both in excruciating pain. And then... ever so slowly... her hand becomes numb, and he stops worrying that his hand is being crushed, and it all passes.*

TOMMY: Is it numb?

ALICE (*quieting down*): ...Yeah.

TOMMY: Cool. Good. Cool.

> *Short pause.*

You don't have to keep squeezing my hand. Or— I mean, you can. I don't know.

> *She lets go.*

Can I, um... I'm just gonna look at it for a second, okay?

> *TOMMY very delicately pulls her hand out of the water.*

Ooohh yeah. You've got a couple second degree burns. And then like, the rest of your hand is basically one big first degree burn. But we'll put Band-Aids on the second degree ones and the rest of your hand should be fine. But just. You know. Don't spill any more coffee on it... please.

ALICE: Thanks.

> *He puts her hand back in the bucket.*

TOMMY: I'm gonna go see if Edzo needs some help. And then I'll come back and check on you. / Okay?

ALICE: Hey... What did you say about— that thing you told me last time.

TOMMY: What thing?

ALICE: About how the first 35 hours someone's gone? How that's "the time"? To find them?

TOMMY: Oh, we don't have to— that was nothing.

ALICE: What was it?

TOMMY: Um... It's just like, in the first 48 hours, after someone um, is when you have like, a 90% chance of finding them.

ALICE: What about after six days?

TOMMY: Oh, that's not— your situation is, like, a totally different situation.

ALICE: I read it drops to less than five percent.

TOMMY: Yeah. But I think it depends on... factors. A lot of factors.

> *Slight pause.*

ALICE: Do you still have those flyers?

TOMMY: Um. I can make more on my break? If you want?

> *Slight pause.*

TOMMY (CONT'D): And hey... you know, my mom and I are gonna do this like, holiday dinner thing at our apartment tonight. Just, if you have no other plans...

ALICE: Oh. Thanks but, I / can't—

TOMMY: I know, yeah. It's stupid. It's...

> *Pause.*

...But like, it would only be for an hour... like a quick hour.

ALICE: I don't think / I'll have—

TOMMY: And I can help you put up posters after. But, just... I think sometimes it's important to take an hour...

> *Blackout.*

SCENE 11

THE LIVING ROOM

That night. ALICE is fervently looking at her phone. DAVE is taping up Christmas lights around the room.

DAVE: There! Alright. Alright. Y'all want to see something amazing? Check it out!

> *DAVE turns off the room lights and plugs in the Christmas lights. They're fine.*

What do y'all think?!

TOMMY: It's great.

DAVE: Yeah, yeah... it is great. Can you believe these weren't even working when I found them in the closet... And then I happened.

> *He marvels at them for a moment.*

I'm going to get some more tape.

> *DAVE bolts out the door.*

TOMMY: So that's my therapist... Are you okay?

ALICE: Yeah. Fine. I think I'm gonna go.

TOMMY: Oh.

ALICE: It's okay. I just— I should be at home right now.

TOMMY: Did you get like a text or something?

ALICE: No. But... there's also the landline and the internet and a million other ways that someone could get word to the house. And I'm not at my house. So...

TOMMY: Okay, but—

> *ANNE and DAVE come in carrying a couple Christmas presents.*

ANNE: Okay, we're only waiting on the French Toast now, shouldn't be long. But I figured now might be... what? What's wrong?

TOMMY: Uh, / she has—

ALICE: Sorry. I actually can't stay for dinner.

ANNE: Well... but I already cooked for four.

ALICE: I just have a— a lot of work to do. At home.

ANNE: Who's making you work this late, it's like eleven. Like Starbucks work?

TOMMY: Mom.

ANNE: Why don't you at least stay for the presents and then after you can decide if you have to work or not.

ALICE: The, presents?

ANNE: Oh— yeah. We just— 'cause every year we're usually working on Christmas Eve and Christmas and so forth? So we trade a couple presents like a week before.

ALICE: ...You got me a present?

ANNE: Of course. Everyone gets one. It's a rule. So you have to at least stay for that.

    (Tiny pause)

Besides, you're like the first person Tommy's brought home in four years. So.

TOMMY: That's wildly *inaccurate*.

ANNE: If you don't want one though / we don't—

ALICE: No, no. It's not... yeah. I can stay.

ANNE: Great! Do we all wanna sit down then? I'll go ahead and start. So, now, I never said it would be a good present, but given the short notice I think it came out alright in the kitchen. This one's for our guest—

TOMMY: No. It's— I got it.

ANNE: What?

TOMMY: I mean I... I already— I have something.

    (Mumbles)

For her.

ANNE: Well where is it?

TOMMY (*whispering*): It's— Mom! I have it, okay? I have it! Don't worry.

ANNE: Why are you whispering?

TOMMY: Mom!

ALICE: You didn't have to get me anything.

TOMMY: It's okay, it's crappy. Or— it's not crappy, it's... you'll see it...

    (Pause)

... Hey-so-can-we-start-or?

ANNE: Alright. I guess I'll go with my other present then. This one's for David.

        She hands him a present.

DAVE: Heeeyy... you didn't have to get me anything.

ANNE: Oh whatever it was only 15 dollars. Or like 25 dollars or 30 or something.

        He starts to open it.

ANNE (*spoiling it*): It's oils. Sorry. It's painting oils.

DAVE (*finally opening it*): Heeeeey.

ANNE: Is that the good kind? I didn't know. Janet from the art section at work said they were good, but I always feel like she lies to me so I wasn't sure...

DAVE (*actually touched*): Thank you. This is really nice.

ANNE (*blushes*): ... Okay. Who's next? Tommy you go.

TOMMY: Okay. So this isn't like a big thing or anything, but.

>*TOMMY grabs a small present and gives it to ALICE. She opens it.*

ALICE: A Michael Buble CD... wow.

DAVE: Oooh he's great.

TOMMY: It's a— It's just the CD case. The actual CD is like a compilation of some pretty good cello songs I put together. It's just a— it's a stupid joke.

ALICE: It's funny.

ANNE: That's really funny, sweetheart.

TOMMY: It's an inside joke.

ANNE: I can still think it's funny... Okay. Next person. Who's next?

DAVE: Uuuhhhh I'll go.

ANNE: Oh, wait! I actually— sorry. Can I go again?

TOMMY: You can't go twice.

ANNE: Yeah but this is from the both of us.

DAVE: It is?

ANNE: Well, you helped me with it so technically it's from the both of us.

>*ANNE picks up a big, flat present.*

  Okay, this one... is for my baby.

TOMMY: Oh no.

ANNE: It's not underwear, so, I'm not gonna embarrass you in front of your...

>*Vague gesture to ALICE.*

TOMMY: OKAY can you just give it to me so I can open it? Okay.

>*She does. He opens it to reveal an art collage. TOMMY looks at the pictures.*
>
>*His brother and him as kids.*
>
>*His brother graduating from high school. His brother making faces at the camera. His brother avoiding the camera.*
>
>*His brother going off to college. His brother not coming back.*
>
>*His brother staring at him.*

ANNE: What do you think?

TOMMY: ...

ANNE: I was talking to David about wanting to do something really artistic, right? And when he told me all the different things I could do I realized that I really wanted to do something for your brother. And they had this collage one that's all about your memories. But when I finished it really didn't feel all that, um *complete.* And I realized that it was because I was missing *your* memories and I thought, what a great thing for us to do together. You know? We can fill it out... you okay?

> *TOMMY's eyes have welled with tears. He's suddenly embarrassed.*

TOMMY: Yeah, I'm— yeah.

> *He stands suddenly.*

ANNE: Oh heeey it's okay.

TOMMY: I know I just gotta...

ANNE: No babe its okay, just let it go. You don't have to be embarrassed.

TOMMY: I'm not.

ANNE: People cry, its okay to cry.

> *Beat.*

Come here.

> *She hugs him.*

> *Then he moves away from her.*

TOMMY: What even is this thing?

ANNE: It's just a, project we can do together. To, you know, to commemorate.

TOMMY: To commemorate what?

ANNE: To commemorate him.

TOMMY: By making a *collage?*

ANNE: Well... it's an artistic project.

TOMMY: Okay?

ANNE: 'Cause it's— 'cause he was really artistic, and... I don't know.

TOMMY: You don't know?

ANNE: I just— I just wanted to do something for him, you know?

TOMMY: ???

ANNE: And— it's just an artistic project / that we can do—

TOMMY: You already said that.

ANNE *(to Dave):* Am I explaining this right? I feel like I'm...

> *DAVE does NOT think this present was a good idea.*

DAVE: Oh, I... yeah that's the basic idea, but.

ANNE: I just wanted us to be able to do something together. I feel like this is something he would've done.

TOMMY: Not like this.

ANNE: Not like what?

TOMMY: He just— agh nevermind.

ANNE: What do you mean?

TOMMY: No nevermind, nevermind let's just move on.

ANNE: Babe it's okay to be upset.

TOMMY: I'm not upset! And you're making it so much worse by saying it out loud like that, / again!

ANNE: Well you're clearly upset / about—

TOMMY: Because he wasn't a fucking art project!

> *(Beat; correcting)*

He's not an art project. And you're foisting this on me like it's this FUN like get together thing.

ANNE: I didn't say it was a get / together thing.

TOMMY: And showing these people this like super personal stuff of his.

ANNE: It's not personal. It's—

TOMMY: It's pictures! It's, it's his stuff and you're showing it to like the world.

ANNE: Why is that bad?

TOMMY: 'Cause there's not much here! It's empty! Like this is all that's left and there's like... it doesn't even cover a fucking poster!

> *He's right. The poster is WAY too big for the small number of pictures and mementos.*

ANNE: So you're mad 'cause... I didn't do a good enough job?

TOMMY: No, I—

> *Tears start to well up again.*

Hoo okay. I gotta, um—

ANNE: Wait, where are you going?

TOMMY: I don't know.

ANNE: Babe, it's okay.

> *She hugs him.*

TOMMY: Stop! I don't want to be hugged.

> *She tries again.*

I don't want to be hugged! Stop!

ANNE: Okay well what do you want?

TOMMY: Can you let go of me please?

> *She doesn't want to.*

Can you please let go of me.

> *She still doesn't.*

Let go of me!

> *She does, TOMMY leaves.*

ANNE: Tommy!

> *ANNE stands there, guilt washing over her.*

Shit.

SCENE 12

THE STREETS OF THE NEIGHBORHOOD

TOMMY's just left his house from the previous scene is wandering around. He's got his coat on.

He's still cold though.

He has no idea where he's going.

He comes upon a street light with a MISSING poster on it for Alice's mom. The tape on one of the corner's lost its adhesive.

He tries to put it back and smooth the tape down, but it won't stay. He tries again.

He's gonna try again, but... he gives up.

He stands there in the cold by himself. It starts to snow.

SCENE 13

THE STARBUCKS BREAK ROOM

TOMMY is alone. ALICE suddenly rushes in, still in her street clothes.

TOMMY: Hey.

ALICE: Hi. Sorry. I know. I know. Sorry.

TOMMY: It's okay.

ALICE: Didn't think I was going to be this late.

TOMMY: It's cool. Is everything okay?

ALICE: Yeah. Just... it's fine. Did you have to call anybody to fill in?

TOMMY: No. It was actually... it was actually pretty cool. It was just me and Edzo? And like, I've totally gotten his lingo down now? So we were just turnin' and burnin' all morning.

ALICE (*impressed?*): Wow... Okay.

> *TOMMY smiles.*

Is he the only one out there right now?

TOMMY: Yeah. But it's pretty quiet. I'm just on my fifteen.

ALICE: Okay.

> *She starts putting on her apron. Long pause.*

TOMMY: Sorry about the other night.

ALICE: Oh don't— it's cool.

TOMMY (*too loud?*): We usually have a lot more fun than that! Ha.

> *ALICE smiles.*

Did you get home okay?

ALICE: Yeah, yeah.

TOMMY: Cool, good.

> *Pause.*

Hey. Um. So when I got in this morning, I made a new batch of posters for tonight? I figured after we close we could go?

ALICE: Oh. Um—

TOMMY: Or we could go tomorrow night if tonight's not, you know.

ALICE: I actually don't... need, to go. Anymore.

> *(Slight pause)*

My mom came back last night.

TOMMY: *What?*

ALICE: That's why I was so late this morning.

TOMMY: Oh my God! How? That's great!

ALICE: I got a call from this guy at a La Quinta Inn. Who was like. "Hey. There's this woman here who keeps asking for people who don't work here. It's really weird. Please come pick her up before I call the cops."

TOMMY's phone starts ringing. He immediately silences it.

TOMMY: Oh my God. How did he know it was your mom?

ALICE: He lives in our neighborhood. And had a couple flyers on his door.

Short pause.

TOMMY: Well— wait, so what are you doing here? Go home! Edzo and I got it covered.

ALICE: No. My aunt drove down this morning, so she's watching her right now. Also this afternoon is the only time the District Manager is free to meet.

TOMMY: Why are you meeting with the DM?

ALICE: I need to talk about taking some time off.

TOMMY: Yeah. Good. Yeah, you should take a while off.

ALICE: Yeah... I'll probably be taking more than a while.

TOMMY: Great. Yeah. Like... how much of a while?

ALICE: I don't know... probably a really long while.

TOMMY: But not like you're quitting though, right?

(Pause)

Are you quitting?

ALICE: I just need to re-assess a lot of things.

TOMMY: Oh.

ALICE: My aunt's gonna come live with us for a while. So... you know? I / just don't—

TOMMY (*devastated*): Great. No yeah that's great. That's really great. Taking time and re-assessing...

(Pause)

Well I'll make sure to hold your spot at work, so don't even, you don't even need to worry about that.

ALICE: Thanks.

She turns to go. But stops

My aunt, um... wanted me to thank you, by the way.

TOMMY: Your aunt?

ALICE: Yeah. She um... didn't know how bad my mom had gotten. She was pretty pissed that I hadn't reached out to her. But she was glad that you were here to help. So... she just wanted to thank you.

TOMMY: Yeah... she's welcome.

> *Pause. They stare at each other for a moment.*

ALICE: Okay. Um. I'm gonna go make sure Edzo isn't fucking anything up. See you out there?

TOMMY: Yeah.

> *She leaves. TOMMY's left alone. He looks at the posters he made for Alice's mother for a moment. Then quietly puts them in the trash.*

SCENE 14

THE WALMART BREAK ROOM

Some shitty Walmart music is playing. Like Nickelback. Or Taylor Swift maybe. Or hell, it's Christmas, maybe something Christmas-y... Anyway. DAVE is standing there. Waiting. Then TOMMY rushes in.

TOMMY (*out of breath*): Hey.

DAVE: Hey.

TOMMY: Um. They said she was back here?

DAVE: Yeah, she just, she's in the manager's office for a sec.

TOMMY looks out the door.

Everything's fine.

TOMMY: There was a fight? Or—

DAVE: No no no, it wasn't a fight.

TOMMY: That's what they said.

DAVE: I mean... okay it was sort of a fight.

TOMMY: My mom got into a *fight?*

DAVE: It's not as bad as it sounds.

TOMMY: With who?!

DAVE: Just another employee, not like a customer or anything.

TOMMY: How is that better?

DAVE: I don't know...

TOMMY: Oh my God. I— where's the manager's office?

DAVE: No no, it's cool. I talked to them already.

TOMMY: What?

DAVE: The General Manager? Patty? I talked to her. We sort of uh, came up together in the electronics department way back when? So. We had a little "chat."

TOMMY: Oh.

DAVE: Yeah... Besides, the guy she got into a fight with is kind of a dick. So...

TOMMY: And she's okay? / She's...

DAVE: Yeah, yeah.

TOMMY (*sincere*): Good... good. Thanks.

(*Short pause*)

Wait, why... are you here?

DAVE: What?

TOMMY: Did they call you? What are you doing here?

DAVE: Oh— no. I was actually gonna talk to your mom on her lunch break.

TOMMY: Why?

DAVE: Rachel called me back.

TOMMY: What?

DAVE: Yeah. We had a LONG talk. She said she was surprised I'd actually showed initiative for once. And also that she hates Houston and would be, "interested in coming back here and seeing how things go."

TOMMY: Oh my God.

DAVE: Yeah.

TOMMY: That's amazing.

DAVE: Yeah.

TOMMY: And so... you said yes, right?

DAVE: I said "yes" like eighteen times. And then I said it like four more times. Because I've been waiting for that call. You know? That call that means everything's going to fit back together the way it used to. And life would become bright. And perfect. And safe. And magical. And it was. For like... six minutes. But then I started to get this... sick, feeling in my stomach. And it was right around when she was congratulating me on finally reaching adulthood at 34-years-old and no longer acting like a 3-year-old that I sort of recognized like, "Oh... You're not a very good person." And she was like, "What?" And I realized I'd said that out loud. So I hung up real quick. And had a heart-attack.

TOMMY: What?

DAVE: Yeah.

TOMMY: Did you call her back?!

DAVE: Nope!

TOMMY: Wait, so... what??

DAVE: I don't know man... When she left? I was all "I'm gonna wait right here for you baby! FOREVER!" And I had this picture in my head of like— I'd be standing here, waiting. Like on a dock or something. Like Ryan Gosling in The Notebook. Building houses and things. Fighting in wars. Then one day she comes back and I'm like, "I've been waiting this whole time." And we take off our shirts. And all this—

> *Motions to his stomach.*

—is just like, chiseled. And we die together holding hands... But in reality I just like, gained 10 pounds. And slept on my friend's couch for a couple months... And I didn't used to be that guy. You know? I used to be happy. I used to have an apartment... so now I gotta figure out what I want to do with my life, since it's not gonna be Rachel.

TOMMY: And you came to my *mom* for that??

DAVE: She's the one who gave me my first job as a therapist. She's the one who helped me get promoted from cash register to the electronics department here. I don't really know what I want to do now ... but I feel like your mom might have some ideas.

TOMMY: Well... we're still gonna meet this Monday though, right?

DAVE: ...You still want to meet?

TOMMY: We haven't finished our ten sessions. I figure we can at least do that.

> *ANNE appears in the doorway. She's holding an ice pack in her hand.*

DAVE: Hey, how you feeling?

ANNE: Okay.

> *(To Tommy)*

What are you doing here?

DAVE: Um... I'm gonna go talk to Patty for a second. Make sure everything's okay.

> *DAVE leaves.*

ANNE: I told him he didn't have to call you.

TOMMY: Mom. What happened?

ANNE (*innocent*): Nothing.

TOMMY: Really? Because that's not what Dave just said. Want to know what Dave just said?

ANNE: No.

> *She walks into the room. She's limping on one leg.*

TOMMY: What happened to your leg?!

ANNE: I just fell, it's nothing.

TOMMY: You're literally limping.

ANNE: Guess what, I'm *old*. Sometimes I limp.

TOMMY: Oh my God. Okay, sit down. Sit down.

> *ANNE sits down. TOMMY kneels in front of her, checking out her knee. Maybe he grabs a few paper towels to wrap the ice pack. He holds it to her knee.*

TOMMY: Who'd you get into a fight with?

ANNE: Nobody.

> *Shakes her head like this is stupid.*

I was on lunch and I was, you know, buying some stuff for you. And Ted was— he was subbing on the register— and when he was checking me out he made this comment like he was joking— but he really wasn't joking—

ANNE (CONT'D): I was buying you some more pop-tarts and he made this comment that was like... do your kids ever get tired of eating the same thing?

She gets really upset by this.

And then he laughed in my face, like it was this big hilarious thing. And so— I might've said a couple things to him that I'm not gonna repeat. And then he said a couple things back that were really rude that I'm also not gonna repeat, and so I said some other things, and then he started yelling and causing a scene! And making it seem like he was this big victim, so. Then, I might've... hit him.

TOMMY: You *hit* him?

ANNE: Just a little bit.

TOMMY: Mom!

ANNE: It was just like a little whack in the arm.

TOMMY: You *whacked* him??

ANNE: It wasn't like I punched him or anything! I just whacked him a little.

TOMMY: You can't do either of those things!

ANNE: Well he was calling me a bad mother, what was I supposed to do?! And you should've seen the things he was doing too. I wasn't the only one looking like an idiot. HE looked like a huge idiot as well, causing scenes and making a ruckus in front of ALL the customers— and he made me fall and hit my ankle, so it's not like this is a one-sided deal here.

TOMMY: Yeah... that doesn't mean you can hit your supervisor though.

ANNE: ... I just really hated the way he laughed. Like I was this horrible person. And everyone laughed with him. Like they all knew. Like it was this big joke they were all in on.

Pause.

I don't know what I'm doing. I'm sorry sweetheart.

TOMMY: It's okay.

ANNE: Is it? I don't know. It doesn't feel okay. It feels like, you know... I had all these people around me once. I had friends and your dad and you and your brother. I had all these people and then I blinked.

TOMMY: Yeah.

ANNE: And I'm so worried that I'm gonna blink again. And you're not gonna be here either.

TOMMY: Where am I going?

ANNE: Where did anybody go?

(Beat)

Is there something wrong with me?

TOMMY: No.

ANNE: Your brother didn't like me very much.

TOMMY: He didn't like a lot of people.

ANNE: I'm not a lot of people.

TOMMY: Well... he would've liked this.

ANNE: Punching Ted and getting fired?

TOMMY: *Yeah.*

ANNE: Shut up, nuh-uh.

TOMMY: Every time you were kept late or they reprimanded you for your clothes or made you work 39.5 hours a week so you'd miss health insurance he'd just be like, "Fuck those people dude."

ANNE: You never told me that.

TOMMY: If he was here right now, he would totally go down to the cashier aisle himself and like, and like, *seek Ted out.*

ANNE (*smiling*)**:** No, come on.

TOMMY: He would bust through the automatic doors and be like, "TED!"

> *ANNE laughs.*

He'd be like "TED! SHOW YOURSELF!"

ANNE: Ted would hide under his register.

TOMMY: Yeah, yeah. And then he'd find him. He'd find Ted and be like "Apologize." And Ted'd be like,

> *(High- pitched)*

"But my snack section." And he'd be like, "Apologize!" And Ted would be like,

> *(High-pitched)*

"You apologize."

ANNE: Or like,

> *(In a shitty voice)*

"You need a coupon if you want to get the discount."

TOMMY: Yeah, and he'd be like, "Here's your discount BRO!" And then he'd take Ted's snack section, and just start wreckin' shit!

ANNE (*covering mouth/laughing*)**:** Oh my God.

TOMMY: Crushin' bags of Skittles. Poppin' Frito bags. Taking snickers and launching them into the kids section like 3-pointers!

ANNE: Like a quarterback!

TOMMY: Yeah! Or— sure.

ANNE: Or like a pitcher!

TOMMY: And then security would come. And you would be like, "What the hell do we do now?" And he would throw you on his back like Spiderman and sprint out of the door!

ANNE: Yeah and I'm real light, so he can do that.

TOMMY: And then he would find Ted's car. And kick in the windshield! And y'all would tear off out of there! And there would be like, everybody would be like chasing you!

ANNE: And, and then we would pick you up from your Starbucks.

TOMMY: Yeah, and I'd jump in the backseat while the car was still moving! 'Cause there'd be like, freakin' helicopters and the FBI behind us!

ANNE: Yeah. And then we'd all go get Burger King!

TOMMY: Yeah. And then we'd stop in Burger King.

ANNE: 'Cause I actually do have some coupons there.

TOMMY: Right. And I'd get a Whopper Jr. meal. And he'd get a Whopper meal. And you'd get a spicy chicken sandwich.

ANNE: No, I just want a Diet Coke.

TOMMY: You'd just get a Coke. And we'd sit there. And eat our meals. And you'd drink your drink. And we'd have to hide in plain sight. Pretending like we were a normal family. Who wasn't being chased by the FBI and their helicopters.

ANNE: Yeah...

> *Pause.*

TOMMY: Or maybe he wouldn't have done any of that. Maybe he would've shown up and just smiled. And been glad, knowing that he wouldn't have to worry about you working at Walmart anymore. Even though he probably wouldn't ever let you know it.

> *They stare at each other for a moment.*

How does your leg feel?

ANNE: Numb.

> *She tidies herself. Smooths her hair down.*

Ted and the rest of the cashiers are probably out there, getting ready to give us death stares as we leave. Do I look okay?

TOMMY: You look great.

ANNE: Wanna help me up?

TOMMY: Yeah.

> *He does. They start to walk out. She grabs his shoulder.*

ANNE: I'm gonna have to lean on you, is that okay?

TOMMY: Yeah.

> *TOMMY helps his mom walk out.*

SCENE 15

TOMMY'S BEDROOM; NIGHT

A laptop opens up, the light illuminating TOMMY's face. He's sending a video message.

TOMMY: Hey. Hey. Or— hold on.

He messes with the camera.

Okay. Yeah. Hey! Hey. Sorry I haven't updated in a couple days, or... weeks. Things have been all like... sorta crazy. Around here. Um... I got some good news though! Guess who the new Shift Supervisor at the Starbucks on Kirkendahl and Louetta is suckaaaaaaaa?

(Pause)

Me. It's me. Which means I have authority now! Um, good news part two: Mom finally quit working at Walmart! Slash, mom got fired from Walmart. Which I know you've been pulling for, for a long time. So you can cross that thing off your list. But, that leads me to good news part three: Um... Mom and I have been talking. And, we think that it might be a good idea to actually... move, away. I mean, not "move away" move away. Just like, "across town to a smaller place" away. We're just not sure that we need all the space... anymore. And what with her trying to find a new job and everything. So... I just wanted to let you know that, I'm not sure where we're gonna be exactly, but it won't be here. So... if you find that you're lonely and need someone to talk to, you might walk into your nearest Starbucks. And maybe when you walk inside, it'll look exactly like my Starbucks. And maybe when you go up to order you'll see a barista behind the bar that looks a whole lot like you, but a little bit younger. And maybe if you ask him for a recommendation of what to get, the barista will have a very limited idea of what to say because he still hasn't learned quite all the drinks yet, even though he's trying very very hard... And so maybe I'll see you around somewhere... but. Maybe I won't... Either way.

TOMMY stares into his laptop for a moment. Then closes it. End of play.

EVERYTHING IS
SUPER GREAT

PROP LIST

- Laptop
- Pop-tarts
- Starbucks Cup
- Clipboard / Sheet
- Make-up (blush or eyeliner)
- Box of muffins.
- Plastic water bottle
- Plastic bag of art supplies (colored pencils, markers, construction paper, notebook paper)
- Dave's notebook
- Joint / Blunt
- Lighter
- Whipped Cream Bottle
- Two cell phones
- Light up and Audible Santa Claus Face
- A stack of Missing Person flyers
- Lots and lots of un-inflated balloons
- A Sharpie marker
- A can of Diet Coke
- A manila envelope
- Pictures, letters, and bank statements of Anne's son
- Bucket of ice
- Christmas lights
- A wrapped present of a CD
- A wrapped present of painting oils
- A poster collage of pictures
- Ice pack

STEELE SPRING
STAGE RIGHTS

ABOUT STAGE RIGHTS

Based in Los Angeles and founded in 2000, Stage Rights is one of the foremost independent theatrical publishers in the United States, providing stage performance rights for a wide range of plays and musicals to theater companies, schools, and other producing organizations across the country and internationally. As a licensing agent, Stage Rights is committed to providing each producer the tools they need for financial and artistic success. Stage Rights is dedicated to the future of live theatre, offering special programs that champion new theatrical works.

To view all of our current plays and musicals, visit:

www.stagerights.com